Baffled & Blessed

DEBBIE OWENS
WITH SOPHIA MORRIS

WESTBOW
PRESS®
A DIVISION OF THOMAS NELSON
& ZONDERVAN

WestBow Press books may be ordered through booksellers or by contacting:

WestBow Press
A Division of Thomas Nelson & Zondervan
1663 Liberty Drive
Bloomington, IN 47403
www.westbowpress.com
844-714-3454

ISBN: 978-1-6642-1155-1 (sc)
ISBN: 978-1-6642-1157-5 (hc)
ISBN: 978-1-6642-1156-8 (e)

Library of Congress Control Number: 2020921851

Print information available on the last page.

WestBow Press rev. date: 12/03/2020

"From the end of the earth will I cry unto thee, when my heart is overwhelmed: lead me to the rock that is higher than I. For thou hast been a shelter for me, and a strong tower from the enemy."
Psalm 61:2-3

Inspiration for Debbie Owens' song–
"Hear My Prayer"

Contents

Preface

It is a privilege beyond words to see a life lived well. Debbie Owens lived a wonderful and unique God story. We met with Debbie numerous times over a few years in order to capture her incredible story. We tried to capture some of the God moments of her life in this little book.

Debbie Owens lived a beautiful life of music, teaching, and raising three amazing girls. She always talked about how much God blessed her, but never ever bragged about herself. Debbie traveled with Maranatha! Music, singing and writing songs. She wrote the beautiful song, "Hear My Prayer." In addition, Debbie taught music classes and directed musicals at Stoneybrooke Christian School. She brought life and love wherever she went. But her greatest pride and joy in life was her three daughters—Jessica, Natalie, and Abigail.

In addition to blessings, God gave her many challenges. It is said that God gives his toughest battles to his strongest warriors, and that is certainly true of Debbie Owens. Through all the painful and heart-wrenching moments in her life, Debbie chose to fix her eyes on Jesus and allow him to determine her steps. If you knew her, then you know she was full of joy and positivity. No matter what challenges she was dealing with, Debbie would always ask, "How are

YOU doing?" God's grace and strength were so prevalent and visible in her life. It was such an inspiration to see one of God's bravest warriors live life well.

Baffled and Blessed is the story of Debbie's life. It's a life story of baffling moments and feeling undeserved, unwanted, and unknown that led to incredible blessings in the arms of a loving Heavenly Father. Her hope in writing this book was that you would see a more vivid portrait of our loving God and learn how to draw closer to Him in the beautiful mess of this life.

Craig & Sophia Morris

Dedication

To my girls, Jessica, Natalie, and Abigail.

Lord, help them to always create a space for You.
Help them to reach the dreams You have for them.
Help them allow Your joy to fill the empty place.
Cause Your Spirit to fill them with Your everlasting love.
I pray that they will always search for Your wisdom, discernment,
grace, peace, and freedom.

To You, God, be the glory.
Let Your Heavenly perspective put a veil over the hurts we face
on earth.
Amen.

(from Debbie Owens' journal)

Living Legacy

How do you fit into a few words on a page, the profound impact one person made on your life? It feels impossible especially when talking about someone as special as our mother. She was selfless, loving, creative, talented and funny. She was faithful and loyal and kind. She was also a mother and our best friend. Throughout our lives, she set a close to perfect example of what it looks like to trust God in every season and through any obstacle. Although our mother left this earth far too soon, she made a powerful and lasting impact with her family, friends, students and even strangers. She will never be forgotten because of the way she made people feel, because of her unwavering faith and her beautiful music. We hope you read this small part of her story and feel encouraged to live a life which focuses on finding true joy in the midst of even the hardest circumstances.

We love you, mom.
Jessica, Natalie & Abigail

Rushing Water

"I don't know if I can make it."

———◆———

"I have told you all this so that
you may have peace in me.
Here on earth you will have
many trials and sorrows.
But take heart, because I have
overcome the world."
Jesus (John 16:33)

G od moments happen in all of our lives, all the time. We don't always notice them or recognize them as God moments. Sometimes they come at an unexpected time or in an unexpected way. Whether we recognize them or not, God regularly creates opportunities for His presence and perspective to shape our lives, guiding us on the journey of life towards heaven.

As I reflected on the strange yet wonderful path God has led me down, He gave me a vision. This vivid image is one I have deeply reflected on, time and time again. I believe God gave me this image as a gift. It has served as a framework for me to walk through dark days with a light inside that could only have come from God. This image has allowed me to…

accept the unacceptable

embrace the incomprehensible

conceive the inconceivable

understand the incomprehensible

conquer the seemingly insurmountable challenges in life.

I was standing on a tiny rock, mere inches above a raging river. My footing was slippery, and I was terrified. As the river threatened to sweep me away with its strong current, I saw a larger rock almost within reach. I hadn't noticed it before— God must have helped me see it. I took a deep breath and reached for the stone. My feet found solid footing. For just a moment, I felt safe. I continued to stare at the rushing water, growing higher and more forceful by the minute. Just when I thought I was going to be swept away, God showed me another stone to step onto. Though equal in size, this stone felt even more stable than the last. Suddenly, God opened up my eyes to see a path of stepping stones. He had placed stone after stone in front of me, to guide me over the tumultuous waters of life. God was inviting me

*to take a faith journey with Him…and I chose
to say yes.*

Step by step, stone by stone, God has taken my hand and led me across a roaring river of challenges in my life—whether it be difficult circumstances, strife in relationships, or a life-threatening illness, He has been with me every step of the way.

Few would deny that life is full of challenges. And this is nothing new—the Bible is full of stories of people who felt overwhelmed and overtaken by the rough waters of life.

Consider the way Jonah cried out to the Father in desperation. Jonah's cry was passionate and relatable. His words easily could've been spoken by any one of us.

*"In my distress I called to the
Lord, and he answered me.
From deep in the realm of the dead I called
for help, and you listened to my cry.
You hurled me into the depths, into
the very heart of the seas,
and the currents swirled about me; all your
waves and breakers swept over me."*
Jonah 2:1-3

Cancer is one of the many battles I fight. You have a battle to fight, as well. Where is the zip code for your fight? Maybe you or a loved one are wrestling with health challenges. Maybe you have a difficult financial situation that causes anxiety about the future. Maybe you have a broken relationship with a friend or family member that needs healing and restoration.

It doesn't matter if you're fighting a physical, emotional, relational, or spiritual battle—God can be found in the midst of it. I know this to be true. My life is evidence of the beauty that can be found when a humble person simply says yes to God's presence.

For some reason, God has chosen me for a particularly long and difficult battle. Through this fight, He has graciously taught me incredible lessons that have drawn me closer to Him and the life He designed for me. When the crushing waters of life challenge you and threaten to knock you down, I pray that you will find the same stones I did, and walk—with God—across the raging waters.

This book is just a snapshot of the journey God has led me on. It's not a self-help book, nor "seven easy steps for the life you've always wanted." This book is my story, an authentic journey of someone who has been *Baffled and Blessed* by God—every single day.

THE FIRST STONE – LOVE

"I am yours."

"My Trust in God flows out of the experience
of His loving me, day in and day out,
whether the day is stormy or fair, whether
I'm sick or in good health, whether I'm in
a state of grace or disgrace. He comes to
me where I live and loves me as I am."
Brennan Manning

"Y**ou can't carry this baby."**
I'm certain my mother was horrified when she
heard these words from the doctor. My mother
had five children. When she decided she was done bearing
and raising children, she had her tubes tied. To those who

are not familiar with this procedure, doctors surgically alter the fallopian tubes so that having a baby is impossible—or supposed to be. I don't know which message disrupted my mother's soul more— "you are pregnant" or "you can't carry this baby." Thankfully, my mother was an incredibly strong woman. Even at the risk of her own life, she courageously forged ahead and gave birth to little ol' me. It's funny how *Baffled and Blessed* describes not only my journey through life, but also my entrance into it!

> *"We all want to be loved, don't we?*
> *Everyone looks for a way of finding love.*
> *It's a constant search for affection*
> *in every walk of life."*
> Audrey Hepburn

We all long to be the object of someone's attention and affection. Searching for love is a common human experience. Unfortunately, most of us allow the truth of our belovedness to be determined by the opinions of others around us.

Many people can relate to the family environment in which I was raised. My father, following the trend of his generation, seemed to lack the capacity to love deeply. I guess the weight of providing for our family financially somehow superseded the responsibility to provide for our relational and emotional needs.

As most little girls do, I craved the love of my father. I regularly chose to do things that I hoped would elicit that love response. Somehow, I thought bringing him his slippers every night would earn me the love my heart and soul craved.

Even though I was a loving, creative little girl, I felt like an outcast. I was the only Christian in my family. Convinced I wasn't really wanted in the first place, my home environment provided fertile ground for the destructive seeds of insecurity and insignificance to be planted in me. It doesn't take much for these negative messages to take root...a strange look from a parent, an unkind word from a friend, or even just isolation can send our own imagination into a disastrous space which grows these toxic seeds in our lives. Feeling unwanted and unloved is not a good way for someone to venture through life. Thankfully, God nudged me to spend time discovering the power and truth contained in the pages of the Bible. Through His Word, God began to shout loving messages that drowned out the whispers of my insecurity and inadequacy.

I learned to listen to God by just sitting quietly in His presence. The first stone, love, brings us God's message that we belong because we belong to Him. The words "I am yours" are sweet and soothing to my soul. I longed to experience that kind of love and belonging with my earthly father. But instead, I received this message from my Heavenly Father!

I don't know if your journey will look the same, but

here are a few movements in my journey towards listening and connecting with Him. First, God nudged me to create intentional space for Him. Next, I sought Him in the pages of Scripture. It was there that my heart, mind, and soul discovered the stone of love. It was in the Bible that I learned how to receive His love by saying, "I am yours." Consider these powerful words from the prophet Zephaniah:

> *"The LORD your God is with you, the Mighty*
> *Warrior who saves. He will take great delight*
> *in you: in his love he will no longer rebuke*
> *you, but will rejoice over you with singing."*
> Zephaniah 3:17

The root of the Hebrew word for "delight" communicates a message of joy, gladness, and pleasure in something or someone. This passage declares that God loves us and delights in us. The Bible says that God *is* love (I John 4:8), so He loves us. It's easy to think that God only loves us because He is obligated to because of His character. Does He really *want* to love us? Does He really *enjoy* being with us? Somehow God, the creator of the universe, *delights* in us?

Yes, He does indeed! Oh, how this verse made my little heart want to dance!

Have you experienced this kind of relationship with God yet? It is our understanding and experience of this unconditional love that transforms our challenging circumstances into the building of beautiful, godly character traits. When we walk in His love, God molds peace and unshakable courage from our feelings of insecurity and inadequacy.

As we step onto the stone of love, God boldly declares that He loves us and desires to be with us. He tells us through His words and through His actions that *we are loved*. And when we let that soak in, everything changes. Since we are loved not because of what we can do for him, but simply because of whose we are, we can trust Him and lean into His loving arms. "I am yours."

Life truly begins when we live with a tenacious belief that we are loved—not because of what we've done, but because of whose we are.

"Your life is not your own: it belongs to
God. To "be yourself" is to be and do
what God wants you to be and do, knowing
that God created you for a mission
and knows you and your mission
better than you do."
Leonard Sweet

THE SECOND STONE – PERSEVERANCE

"God will sustain us."

"Beginning well is a momentary thing.
Finishing well is a lifelong thing."
Ravi Zacharias

"What are we going to feed the girls?"

That is a terrible thought to wake up to on a Saturday morning. My husband Steve and I had no money and no groceries—but we did have three sweet girls who would be waking up soon and asking for breakfast. As my heart filled with anticipatory grief and sadness, the question echoed in my head— "What are we going to feed them?"

I decided to scrape together some money and go to the

store to get milk for cereal and cream for our coffee. I opened the messy drawer in our kitchen and found a yellow post-it note pad. I wrote down two lonely words:

Milk. Cream.

Tears streamed down my cheeks as I thought to myself, "We don't *need* cream. Cream isn't vital. We just need the essentials."

I stared at that post-it note for thirty minutes. Steve's question broke the silence.

"Did you go to the store?" he asked.

"No." This simple reply came from a deeper place. I wasn't merely sharing information—I was responding with the desperation of a needy heart.

"Did Jessica go to the store?" he inquired.

"No," I solemnly answered again.

Intrigued, he shared, "There is a cold gallon of Alta Dena milk and a pint of half and half on the porch."

I opened the front door and stared in disbelief as the two items I had written on my post-it were now sitting in front of me. Astonished, I looked up and down the street for an answer to this great mystery. I asked the neighbors if there was a milkman who delivered milk in the area. They said no.

I continued to stare up and down the street. I'm not sure what I was looking for. Maybe the milk and cream fairy?

To this day, I have no idea where the milk and cream

came from. I cried again as I added this event to God's credit column. He is so good and so full of grace.

I took this as a whisper of encouragement to continue running the race. God showed me the next step—onto the stone of perseverance. Perseverance is continuing to journey ahead, even when it's difficult. As God continued to write my story, He nudged my heart with His powerful and encouraging words:

> *"For this reason, since the day we heard about you, we have not stopped praying for you. We continually ask God to fill you with the knowledge of his will through all the wisdom and understanding that the Spirit gives, so that you may live a life worthy of the Lord and please him in every way: bearing fruit in every good work, growing in the knowledge of God, being strengthened with all power according to his glorious might so that you may have great endurance and patience, and giving joyful thanks to the Father, who has qualified you to share in the inheritance of his holy people in the kingdom of light. For he has rescued us from the dominion of darkness and brought us into the kingdom of the Son he loves,*

in whom we have redemption,
the forgiveness of sins."
Colossians 1:9-14

In the original language, verse 11 speaks of perseverance in two different ways. One is walking with God's strength through difficult circumstances. The other is walking with God's strength when interacting with difficult people.

Are you in the midst of a difficult circumstance? Are you struggling with difficult people? God's incredible power is available to you! If we embrace God's glorious presence and remember the truth in the message of the Gospel, God will provide for us and sustain us. Sometimes I need to ask for forgiveness when I don't believe that the God who provided His people with a land of milk and honey can provide milk and cream for me.

At some point on our journey, hope will begin to fade, our hard work will meet its end, and perseverance will show up with two really important questions—"Is it worth it? Can I do it?"

Perseverance itself is a journey. It is a battle within a battle. In order to win the fight of your life, you must first win the battle for perseverance.

God's powerful presence is what enables us to persevere. In Joshua 3:7-13, during the time of the exodus from Egypt, the Israelites were preparing to cross into the promised land.

God told the religious leaders to take a step of faith into the rushing water of the Jordan River. God spoke, and they trusted Him. They took that step of faith. When they did, the priests' faith was emboldened, and God proved to be powerful and righteous.

In the same way God miraculously stopped the rushing water of the Jordan River, he still does miracles today. He doesn't always stop the water from rushing over us, but he promises that he will be with us in the midst of it.

> *When you pass through the*
> *waters, I will be with you;*
> *and when you pass through the rivers,*
> *they will not sweep over you.*
> *When you walk through the fire,*
> *you will not be burned;*
> *the flames will not set you ablaze.*
> Isaiah 43:2

The stone of perseverance is also a reminder that I am not alone. If it were not for this rock, I wouldn't be able to stand in the rushing waters. If it were not for God, I wouldn't be able to stand the difficulty this life has thrown at me.

As silly as it is, I have never ever owned the place where I lived. We've moved from renting apartments, to relying on the generosity of godly people to let our family live with them, to renting again. Don't get me wrong, I'm incredibly thankful. And yet, there is an added level of perseverance necessary to trust God to continue to care for our needs—not just the milk and cream, but also the roof over our heads. God is the strength behind my perseverance. When I start to feel frightened, anxious, or worried, I close my eyes and see the God who is always with me—the God of perseverance.

"We can be certain that God will give
us the strength and resources
we need to live through any situation
in life that he ordains.
The will of God will never take us where
the grace of God cannot sustain us."
Billy Graham

THE THIRD STONE – DESIRE

"I am cherished."

"Measure not God's love and
favor by your own feeling.
The sun shines as clearly in the darkest
day as it does in the brightest.
The difference is not in the
sun, but in some clouds
which hinder the manifestation
of the light thereof."
Richard Sibbes

"Whose picture is this?" I asked my husband with a tone of curiosity and dread. While cleaning the attic, I had come across a dusty Father's Day card. I opened it up to find the photo of a child I had never seen.

With a tilted head and a concerned look, I asked my husband Steve what the story was. In a gruff business-like tone, Steve responded, "I didn't think you needed to know."

Didn't think I needed to know?! His curt reply echoed through my head and sliced through my heart. Until a few moments ago, I didn't even know this child existed. And somehow, he didn't think I needed to know about a previous marriage and another child?? I closed my eyes as pain flooded my heart and confusion clouded my mind.

As time passed, I began to understand the motivation behind his secrecy. For years, he lived a lie and hid the truth because of an oppressive fear many of us share—"If you really knew me, you wouldn't love me."

Although I was enraged at the thought of his double life and lack of integrity, there was part of me that was compassionate. I started to make sense of this huge relational blunder by looking at my own life. I, too, have been plagued by the pervasive fear that "If you really knew me, you wouldn't love me." And somewhere along this journey of life, I lost myself.

Deep inside, I'm a "people-pleaser." I've been trying to please others my entire life. There is tension in my heart. The fearful part of me wants to run away from people, while the part of me that yearns for love and connection wants to run towards people. That's kind of silly, isn't it? I am simultaneously hiding myself from others while trying to perform for them.

There was another lie lurking in the background of my life: "If I perform well, I will be loved more." As I shared earlier, when I was a little girl, I brought my dad's slippers to him every night. I desperately hoped that one day he would lavish me with the love my soul craved. He never did.

The years passed, and the game I played to earn love by my performance continued. Once again, I found myself striving for love and connection in a relationship with a man who didn't value relationships. I tried to earn my husband's love to fill the void my father left. I was unsuccessful, and the void remained empty.

Many of us do the same thing. We desperately want to be loved, and we look to others to fill that void. Are you performing for someone in order to earn their love? Is there someone whose love you believe will fulfill you?

Steve was my security. He wanted it that way. He didn't want me—he wanted to leave a legacy. Simply put, he was a slick salesperson. One moment in the attic triggered all my insecurity and doubt. And worst of all, the lies I believed in my head and in my heart continued to grow. I wondered, "If

Steve doesn't love or listen to me, maybe God doesn't love or listen to me either. What if God doesn't hear my prayers?"

Through all my doubts and insecurity, God led me to the stone of desire. He spoke to my soul and told me that *I am cherished.* Did you hear that? Cherished! Through the years of my battle with this disease, I have learned how to listen to God. He *does* listen to our prayers. He *does* speak to us. He has something special to say to each one of us. Are you listening?

If you were near the temple during the time of Jesus's crucifixion, do you know what you would've heard? The sound of a curtain ripping. Matthew gives us a glimpse of what happened at Jesus' death.

> *"At that moment the curtain of the temple*
> *was torn in two from top to bottom.*
> *The earth shook, the rocks split."*
> Matthew 27:51

The sound of the curtain tearing, the sound of rocks splitting, and the sound of Jesus' body breaking for you is God's cosmic declaration that you are desired—you are cherished! Romans 12:2 says, "For the joy set before him, he endured the cross." There was a joy Jesus looked forward to—something he didn't have in heaven, that he would only have on the other side of the cross. Do you know what that something is?

It's you and me. It's almost unfathomable—the king of kings and lord of lords wants to be with us! He wants us just as we are. He desires for us to be with him and to receive the love he lavishes upon us.

If you ever doubt that God desires you, ask yourself this—"What did it take for God to love you? To forgive you? What did it take to tear the curtain of our separation from God?" It took the life and death of the Son of God. The *God of the universe* declared that he wanted us to be with him *forever.* And if being eternally desired by the One who created us doesn't move our hearts, nothing will.

It is the experience and knowledge that I am God's desired one that helps my heart heal from the love I didn't receive from my father or from my husband. God's healing is miraculous when we accept these truths!

Fast forward many years later to a peaceful Saturday morning at home. I was sitting in the kitchen, coffee in hand, simply listening to God. No one else was around. Suddenly, words came pouring out of my mouth: "I love you, too!" These words caught me by surprise. The uncontainable conversation in my soul exploded into a conversation out loud. This truth flashed upon me like lightning on a stormy night, but it was as warm as a cup of hot chocolate next to a fireplace.

God loves me.

He desires to be with me.

I am cherished.

And I love him back.

The words kept flowing from my mouth. "You love me. You love me. You love me." The peace and stillness of the moment seemed to last an eternity as I rested in the love of the Father. I whispered, "I don't understand it, but I accept it."

Challenges are part of the fabric of this life. In the midst of difficult circumstances, when we stand on the unshakable stone of God's eternal desire for us, our lives and our relationships can be transformed. God has spoken desire into your life. He has declared with his words and actions that *you are cherished.* Now you have the choice: Are you going to believe him? Are you going to take Him at His word?

"It's not about finding ways to avoid
God's judgment and feeling like a failure
if you don't do everything perfectly.
It's about fully experiencing God's
love and letting it perfect you.
It's not about being somebody you are not.
It's about becoming who you really are."
Stormie Omartian

THE FOURTH STONE – FAITH

"Okay God, let's do this!"

*"If we will but let our God and
Father work His will with us,
there can be no limit to His
enlargement of our existence."*
George MacDonald

I was sitting in the doctor's office, awaiting the results of a test. A woman in a white coat entered silently, arms folded and head tilted to the side.

"Really? I have cancer?!" I was in shock.

"Yes," she gently replied. "We don't know where it's coming from, but it's there."

I shook my head in disbelief and thought to myself, "And

of all days, today's my birthday!" It's so strange that on the day people were celebrating my birth, I began to think about my death. It seems astounding that a few cells in my body could change the course of my life.

I slowly made my way to the car. My heart and mind were racing. I was caught in a tornado of thoughts and feelings. I opened the door and crumpled into the driver's seat. I sat in silence, crying and questioning God. "Haven't my girls been through enough already? How am I going to tell them?"

I drove a few miles and cried out to God again, "How am I going to do this?"

For some reason, that drive home felt endless. Maybe I hit all red lights. Maybe it's because the value of my time began to change. Finally, through the fog of my muddled thoughts, I made it home safely. I took a deep breath and opened the door. As I stepped inside, the only thing I could think about was, "I have cancer. I have cancer. I have cancer." Yet the only words I heard from my daughters were, "What's for dinner?"

I know my girls. I know they would've cared deeply if I had told them the bad news, but I wasn't ready for that yet. Instead, I did my Debbie thing and shifted into go mode. "I'll run to the store. What sounds good?" Those were the words that came out of my mouth. But within my soul, unspoken words of strife and confusion bubbled at the surface. What a surreal moment—experiencing life in the meaningful and the mundane. "I have cancer…what's for dinner?"

Looking back on it now, I knew something was wrong even before I went to the doctor, I just never thought it could be this big. I was exhausted after directing the elementary school musical at Stoneybrooke in December 2015. But it didn't feel like ordinary fatigue…somehow this was different. Following a rehearsal, I sank into the front pew of the school chapel with one recurring thought in my head: "I really don't feel good. I feel sick."

I had always been very healthy. I would get a little bug now and then, but I was never really sick. I made an appointment with my doctor, but it was last minute so I could only see her PA. I told her I felt like I had the stomach flu. I felt nauseous all the time. My lower back ached and I was always tired. I didn't have a fever. I didn't throw up. I was just nauseous.

She gave me a prescription. That never sits well with me, when the doctor just gives you some medicine but doesn't really know what's wrong. I was also given an order for an ultrasound. "Just in case you feel like you need it," she said. I ignored the "just in case" part and called to schedule the ultrasound as soon as I left the office. Somehow, I knew this illness might be different.

After the ultrasound, I went back to my doctor and she told me they wanted to do more testing. That's not usually a good sign. They wanted to do a CT scan because they saw something in my liver. I completed the scan and returned to get the results. Happy birthday to me—the doctor confirmed that the disease that took my mother in 2008 was floating around in my body as well.

Instead of going to the store, my girls offered to take me out to dinner for my birthday. I really didn't feel like going out...or doing anything, for that matter. But we went anyway. I don't know how I sat through a birthday dinner without falling apart at the thought of the cancer within me.

It's amazing the lengths a parent will go to in order to protect their children from pain. Maybe that's part of our struggle—protecting them from pain versus allowing them to see God in the midst of suffering. I dreaded the moment I would have to tell them. My imagination went wild. I even wondered if I could actually go through chemotherapy without ever telling them about it.

It was a Saturday morning shortly after I found out about my cancer. I was alone at home, cleaning and doing laundry. Out of nowhere, like a flashflood, I couldn't move and began to cry. Tears are a funny thing. Sometimes we let them out. Sometimes God pulls them out. Sometimes they're cute, baby tears. But not these—they were huge, pain-filled, soul tears, fully equipped with wailing and gasping for breath. It was an ugly cry I couldn't control.

Through the blurry sea of tears, I saw that the door of my apartment was open to the balcony. I scrambled to find a pillow to put over my face in order to soften the sound of my wailing. I was legitimately concerned that my neighbors would burst into the apartment, looking for a dying coyote.

We all face sadness, pain, and despair. Where do you go? To whom do you run? My heart is filled with gratitude that God always draws me close to Him. I think this is especially important when we are in pain. No one feels wanted when they are ugly crying. And yet, it seems that pain is necessary to bring us to God with an honest heart.

In this authentic, pain-filled moment, I cried out, "God, it's not that I don't trust you, I'm just so scared!" Suddenly I felt God himself put His hands on my shoulders. He gently guided me to the couch. I usually prefer to stand, but if God wants me to sit, I will. So, I did. I sat and waited. I whispered, "Okay, God—you have my attention."

I still remember what He said to me, word for word— because when God speaks to you, those words are etched on the walls of your soul forever. He spoke in a strong, still voice. He said, "I've got you! And through this, I am going to show your girls who their Heavenly Father is."

The Old Testament recounts the story of a man named Abraham. He was human, fallible, and a man of faith as well. He was offered a stone of faith to step onto, like I was. God asked Abraham to trust Him, and he did. Paul reflects on this story in his letter to the Hebrews:

> *"Now faith is confidence in what we hope for*
> *and assurance about what we do not see.*
> *This is what the ancients were*
> *commended for... By faith Abraham,*
> *when called to go to a place he would later*
> *receive as his inheritance, obeyed and went,*
> *even though he did not know*
> *where he was going."*
> Hebrews 11:1, 8

Abraham was able to leave what was comfortable and familiar, despite his fear of the unknown, because of his trust and faith in God. Abraham didn't know where he was going, but he knew who he was going with.

There I was, sitting on my couch, having a conversation with God. He took me by the hands and led me to the stone of faith by speaking these powerful words to me: "I've got you! And through this, I am going to show your girls who their Heavenly Father is." These words flowed into me with power. That day, God gave me supernatural reassurance of His presence and purpose. My wails were silenced. My tears were wiped away. I sat there for a moment longer, gathering myself. I responded to His call by saying,

"Okay God, let's do this!" I stood up and continued on with my day.

Have I cried since? Absolutely! But have I wailed like a dying coyote in complete fear? No. The stone God gave me was an opportunity to step out of the waters of fear and into a life of faith. The stone of faith is foundational for us to live life according to God's glorious design. The Bible makes it unmistakably clear that He is trustworthy, and that even the faith we have is a gift from Him (Ephesians 2:8-9).

God has given me the opportunity to step onto the solid stone of faith. I have experienced the reality of walking a difficult road with confidence. If God is with me, He will continue to show me the way and give me strength for each step. God offers this same opportunity to you. The friends and family who love you, the marvelous experiences you you've had, and the beauty in the world all point to the gift of faith that He offers us. When we step onto the stone of faith and choose to trust God, He gives us the stability we need to walk well through this life and into the next.

> *"What a sharp pain will go through*
> *us when we suddenly realize that*
> *we could have produced complete and*
> *utter joy in the heart of Jesus*
> *by remaining absolutely confident in*
> *Him, in spite of what we were facing."*
> Oswald Chambers

THE FIFTH STONE – CONFIDENCE

"We've got this."

*"Faith is a living, daring confidence in
God's grace, so sure and certain
that a man could stake his life
on it a thousand times."*
Martin Luther

M ichael W. Smith once sang, "Into every life a little rain must fall." This is so true. Challenges rush towards all of us. Personally, I don't know which storm was worse—finding out I had cancer or having to share that news with my girls. Of course, I had to share the news, but even just the thought of telling them made my stomach churn. Their dad left, we had no money, and I was virtually paralyzed by the fear of being alone and abandoned. I have tried to escape these fears for most of my life, and I desperately wished for my daughters to live without them. But now this? It just didn't seem fair.

I knew the night I shared the news would be an awful evening. I knew I needed relational support, so I told my oldest daughter, Jessica, first. As expected, she received the news with an abundance of uncontrollable tears. We just held each other and cried. Her husband, Kevin, processed the information with a quiet, supportive confidence. I needed them to support me as I shared the hardest speech of my life with my youngest girls.

Jessica and Kevin lived in the same apartment complex, so when the time was right, they came over. I was distracted and fearful. I did my best to delay the inevitable by getting people water and trying to engage in small talk. Kevin's mom, Barbara, was with us that night. She nudged me with her shoulder and gave me that knowing look, indicating that it was time. I needed to be confident and just tell them.

My body went completely numb as I blurted out something like, "Girls, I got the results of my tests back and they found a tumor in my colon. It's cancerous, and it has spread to my lymph nodes and liver." Naturally, there was a rollercoaster of shock, panic, fears, and tears. I was right. It was awful. But somehow, God strengthened me to share what needed to be shared.

Challenges often come like waves in the ocean—one after another after another. As I consider the recent trials in my life, these three phrases came to mind. They pretty much sum up the set of waves that came into my life:

"Dad's leaving."

"I have cancer."

"Dad's gone."

I'm learning that the most important thing isn't what happens to us, it's what happens in us. How we choose to respond, how we interpret the challenges we face, and how we manage the messages in our heads and in our hearts dictates whether we fall apart or fall towards Jesus. God is offering us a new stronghold, a stone of confidence that enables us to see life through his eyes and live with his heart.

On this journey, I have learned how to paint life with different colors. I have learned how to experience the fullness of a broken yet beautiful life. The apostle Paul learned this, too. Listen to the confidence in his words to a struggling church in Philippi:

> "Yes, and I will continue to rejoice, for I know
> that through your prayers and God's provision
> of the Spirit of Jesus Christ what has happened
> to me will turn out for my deliverance. I
> eagerly expect and hope that I will in no way
> be ashamed, but will have sufficient courage so

that now as always Christ will be exalted in my
body, whether by life or by death. For to me, to
live is Christ and to die is gain. If I am to go on
living in the body, this will mean fruitful labor
for me. Yet what shall I choose? I do not know!
I am torn between the two: I desire to depart
and be with Christ, which is better by far; but
it is more necessary for you that I remain in
the body. Convinced of this, I know that I will
remain, and I will continue with all of you
for your progress and joy in the faith, so that
through my being with you again your boasting
in Christ Jesus will abound on account of me."
Philippians 1:18-26

Paul lived his life with great confidence, and I am learning from his example. As I look back at that awful night where I shared the news with my girls, I can see God working powerfully. After the initial shock subsided, with wet Kleenex in hand, I continued. "This sucks, and it isn't going to be easy. But I can't fake the peace you see in me. We've made it through some really tough things and I know God is going to get us through this, too."

We made it through that night, and with God's strength, we've continued to make it. With God's help, we adopted a "we got this" mindset—living one day at a time, learning transformative life lessons, and walking with Jesus. God has shown me another stone to leap onto when the waves threaten me—the stone of confidence. I have confidence because of the One who lives in me. The more I lean on God and trust Him, the stronger He makes me. When we allow Him to rule in our hearts, we can experience an unexplainable strength that only comes from the presence of our Heavenly Father. Wherever it is that you need His strength—in a relationship, in your finances, in your personal life—say yes to the invitation He offers in the form of the stone of confidence.

"But why should we not place implicit
confidence in God and rely upon His word of
promise? Is anything too hard for the Lord?
Has His word of promise ever failed?
Then let us not entertain any unbelieving
suspicions of His future care of us.
Heaven and earth shall pass away,
but not so His promises."
Arthur W. Pink

THE SIXTH STONE – AUTHENTICITY & VULNERABILITY

"I'm going to be me."

"Authenticity is being honest with yourself.
Vulnerability is being honest with others."
Craig Morris

I t's hard to smile when you don't feel like it. I've had almost the same routine every day. Wake up, encourage myself to pretend, and decide to put on a happy face. I adopted the "fake it 'til you make it" operating system for my life. Inevitably, at some point during my day, someone would corner me and share their deepest woes: "My kitchen counters didn't turn out right during our remodel... My son got an A- in his class... I just got my fingernails done and I already broke one!" Their lament was often followed up with, "I'm just beside myself. I don't know what to do!"

My mind drifted to review the facts of my own life: My husband left me. We have no money. My girls are struggling. I have cancer.

I'm afraid at some point my eyes glazed over. I would try to recover by putting on another fake smile, nodding my head, feigning compassion, wondering if they could see through me or if I could really keep this up.

During those days, I learned that it is nearly impossible to have genuine empathy for someone when you're pretending that everything is great. So, I made a deep, soul decision—"I'm going to be me." God led me to the stone of authenticity. I realized the importance of being the real, authentic, genuine me that God created. But in order to be authentic, I had to be vulnerable. Authenticity and vulnerability are two parts of the same stone. Like a conglomerate rock, each part is weak on its own, but together they form a strong foundation.

Authenticity requires knowing our true self. We must hold up the mirror to our heart and soul, not the façade we show the world. Sometimes the road to authenticity begins with finding ourselves for the first time. Many of us grew up in a world that told us who we are, what to do, what to think what to feel, what to say, etc. Now, we must dare to find out who we really are, without the voices and opinions of others. And to do so, we have to ask some difficult questions.

> Am I okay if not everyone loves me? Is it okay if not everyone likes me?

> Why is it so hard to be my true self with others?

> Why do I constantly try to manage the image others see?

> Why do I wear the unrealistic burden of making everyone around me happy?

For some reason, when you have nothing, it's easier to be yourself. Have you ever noticed that people who have struggled with addiction—and won—are some of the most authentic and vulnerable people around? Here is a challenging question we all need to be asking ourselves on a regular basis: What percentage of your true self are you currently sharing with the people around you?

Without question, Jesus was a wise man. John 2:24 tells us that it was His insight that kept Him from sharing 100% of Himself with everyone around Him. I'm not encouraging you to share all of yourself with everyone you meet. I'm simply encouraging you to learn what I've learned—the blessing of sharing who you are with those whom you trust. This step will have a beautiful, positive impact on our lives and relationships.

At first it seems like authenticity and vulnerability requires intentional planning, conscious decisions, and purposeful energy. But after a while, new muscles will grow to allow authenticity to flow smoothly and naturally throughout our relationships.

We have been offered a powerful opportunity. The chance to stand on this stone and declare with our lives and relationships, "I'm going to be me," is a decision that can unlock incredible personal strength. You might be wondering, "What kind of strength?" When we are authentic and vulnerable, God leads us. He fills us with his unfailing strength and reminds us that we are chosen and loved.

When faced with a seemingly unconquerable trial, the apostle Paul stood on the stone of authenticity and vulnerability. He gained strength when heard these words from God:

> *"But He said to me, 'My grace is sufficient for*
> *you, for my power is made perfect in weakness.'*
> *Therefore, I will boast all the more gladly*
> *about my weaknesses, so that Christ's power*
> *may rest on me. That is why, for Christ's*
> *sake, I delight in weaknesses, in insults, in*

hardships, in persecutions, in difficulties.
For when I am weak, then I am strong."
2 Corinthians 12:9-10

The strength of authenticity and vulnerability also appears in the form of freedom. Those who walk in the integrity of being who they truly are walk with an indescribable lightness. Those who are courageous and willing to risk vulnerability can experience the freedom to stop pretending, and the peace of living in honesty.

Authenticity and vulnerability can impact not only us, but the people around us, as well. A generous friend of mine blessed me with the gift of a massage. Thoughtful as it was, I was reluctant to go for many reasons. The biggest reason was the humiliation of having to explain all the broken parts of my body. I scheduled the appointment anyway and stood on the stone of authenticity and vulnerability. I shared everything that was going on with my life and body, and then the massage began.

For some reason, I was prompted to pray for this female masseuse during my massage. When it was over, I tenderly shared, "You know, what you do is really important."

Shocked and unsure, she replied, "Are you sure?"

I nodded my head. "That was amazing." Allowing the authenticity to take over, I added, "The funny thing is, I was praying for you during the massage."

Her eyes got big and a look of surprise came across her face. "I was praying, too! I never pray, but for some reason, I was praying the whole time!"

God had heard my heart. I added the words of encouragement, "God just wanted me to tell you that what you do is important." She hugged me and we went on our way.

This God moment never would have happened if I had continued to fake my life and if I had allowed my self-consciousness to overcome my concern for the things God wanted me to do and say. It is only when we are our true selves that we can be a conduit of God's grace and goodness to the lost and hurting world around us. God rescued us not for ourselves alone, but to help others find the Father who forgives us without limits and loves us endlessly.

"Are you tired? Worn out? Burned
out on religion? Come to me.
Get away with me and you'll recover your life.
I'll show you how to take a real rest.
Walk with me and work with
me—watch how I do it.
Learn the unforced rhythms of grace.
I won't lay anything heavy or ill-fitting on you.
Keep company with me and you'll
learn to live freely and lightly."
Matthew 11:28-30 (MSG)

If this passage moves your soul as it does mine, maybe it's time for you to step onto the stone of authenticity and vulnerability. Because I have taken this step of faith, I can boldly declare, "I am finally who God wants me to be." There are few things better in this world than the feeling of confidence and freedom, knowing that you are living authentically and for the ultimate purpose of serving God.

*"While the impostor draws his identity
from past achievements and the adulation
of others, the true self claims identity in
its belovedness. We encounter God in the
ordinariness of life: not in the search for
spiritual highs and extraordinary, mystical
experiences but in our simple presence in life."*
Brennan Manning

THE SEVENTH STONE – SURRENDER

"It's yours."

*"What Thou wilt. When Thou
wilt. How Thou wilt."*
John Newton

Sometimes we choose surrender. Sometimes surrender chooses us. I still remember with crystal clarity the moment I heard Steve say, "I'm moving to Tulsa. We have two weeks to get out of our apartment. You need to find a place to live." Disbelief crashed into my heart and soul. As these words seeped from his mouth, coldly and smoothly, they brought my worst fears to life. My husband was leaving me all alone, with three kids, no money, and no place to go.

Forsaken.

Dismissed.

Abandoned.

These are powerful feelings that I wouldn't wish on my worst enemy. As my life circumstances shifted, I was caught in a whirlwind of emotions. I closed my eyes to pray and the image God had given me of rushing water reappeared. I was not in the water, but it was rushing all around me, growing stronger and more powerful. I was scared and confused. Just then another stone appeared—surrender. It was a gift, a small place of safety for me to step onto. With one single step, I simultaneously moved towards God, towards health, and towards everything else I wanted.

Don't be mistaken, this was certainly not an easy step to take. This stone called me to leave behind my desire to be in control, my passion to have the appearance of personal strength, and the firm grip I had on wanting to handle things on my own. God was calling me into a new chapter of surrendering my life to Him.

One of the benefits I experienced as I yielded to God and His will was the transformation of my perspective. In the past, I looked at life through one lens, focusing on everything I was losing. Standing on the stone of surrender, I began to see through a different lens. It was on this stone that I discovered that I have had everything and nothing at the same time. I had virtually no possessions, yet I possessed the greatest One of all. Jesus is what my heart and mind focused on and wanted more than anything else.

Like Paul, I have learned the secret of contentment. Unlike what our culture whispers to us, contentment flows through a person, not a possession or an experience. Paul challenges us with these words:

> "Keep your lives free from the love of money
> and be content with what you have,
> because God has said, "Never will I
> leave you; never will I forsake you."
> Hebrews 13:5

True surrender happens when we acknowledge our limitations and embrace God's limitlessness. Surrender doesn't mean giving up. Quitters give up. Winners surrender what is uncontrollable to the One who orchestrates the universe. There is a big difference between saying "uncle" and throwing in the proverbial towel versus saying "daddy" and throwing ourselves into God's loving arms. When we surrender ourselves, our dreams, and our lives to the One who created and sustains the whole universe, warm contentment flows through us. Contentment comes from companionship— specifically, a deep relationship with Jesus. I have embarked on a journey of learning how to surrender my own dreams and let God lead me to *His* dreams for me. And if I can do this, you can, too!

I've gotten used to relinquishing my possessions. In fact, everything I own fits in a two-bedroom apartment. But as hard as it is to give up my earthly possessions, watching my body deteriorate has been even harder. For some reason, hair, eyelashes, and fingernails seem to slowly disappear when battling cancer. Pulling clumps of hair out of your head is a strange experience, to say the least. It's interesting how life can be a sort of living horror movie with threads of beauty woven throughout. This is what life on the stone of surrender is like—having everything and nothing, all at the same time.

"It's yours," is one of the banners I have flown over my life. It is the same message that flowed over the life of Christ. Philippians 2 reflects how Jesus emptied himself of the glory He had in heaven and became a servant, solely because he wanted a relationship with me and you. That is incredible news! When we stand firmly on the stone of surrender, our understanding and experience of God completely changes our lives.

> *"Just as water ever seeks and*
> *fills the lowest place,*
> *so the moment God finds you*
> *abased and empty,*
> *His glory and power flow in."*
> Andrew Murray

THE EIGHTH STONE – GRACE

"I am Worthy & Undeserving."

*"This notion that grace is healing omits
the fact that before it heals, it cuts with the
sword Christ said He came to bring."*
Flannery O'Connor

Small things can feel like an enormous burden when you have cancer. I've learned that God can handle life when big, bad things happen. But what about the smaller things in life? Like a car breaking down? Can he handle that, too? We had one car in our family. And it was essential, as the link between teaching voice lessons, a music class, and doing everything I could to put food on the table and provide a decent life for my girls.

One day, my car broke down. It was just a cherry on top of all the other sandbags of life that were weighing me down. I didn't realize that something as small as the breakdown of my car could break me down, too.

I took the car to the shop and they gave me an estimate for the repairs. My face flushed as I realized it would cost more money than I had and more money than I make. This was one of those "end-of-the-rope" moments when I couldn't understand how challenge after challenge could coexist with the promise that God was working all things for good (Romans 8:28).

Somehow, news got out and a gracious family heard about my predicament. They called the auto shop and paid for my car to be fixed. When I heard that the repairs were paid for, strange feelings collided in my heart. I felt a combination of extreme gratitude and deep shame. I was thankful for their amazing generosity, but embarrassed about the situation I was in. Once again, terrible feelings of dependence and unworthiness crept in.

It was at that moment that God showed me the next stone He had made available to me—grace. Sometimes we can see the next step, and sometimes we need others to help us see where God is leading us. This family helped me take a step onto the stone of grace. And as I did, I learned some extraordinary lessons about life and faith.

The dictionary definition of grace is "undeserved favor." That's a nice definition, and grace is a beautiful word. But it doesn't even come close to capturing the magnitude of the collision of feelings one experiences when they simultaneously feel blessed and undeserving.

Through my broken car, God whispered a message of grace to my broken heart. He said, "You can't afford to fix your car—but you're going to get it fixed anyway. And You can't afford to fix your own soul—but you're going to get it fixed anyway." This message reminded me that I don't deserve God's grace because of my actions, but I am worthy of it because I have been made in His image. When we stand on the stone of grace, we simultaneously declare, "I am undeserving" and "I am worthy."

Above the waterline, visible part of the rock is where the failures and inadequacies of our lives slap at our ankles. These messages constantly remind us that we are human and prone to making mistakes. It won't help us to ignore these messages. In fact, paying attention to these messages is what drives us deeper into the grace of God. As Jonathan Edwards once shared, "You contribute nothing to your salvation except the sin that made it necessary." Acknowledging that our behavior has missed the mark, and will continue to miss it, allows us to be more confident in the reckless and relentless grace of God.

Underneath the rushing current, the part of the stone that

is unseen yet steadfast is the foundation of our worthiness. A little boy who makes a sailboat, loses it, and then finds it again proclaims, "Little sailboat, you are twice mine! For I have made you and I have redeemed you." Similarly, our worthiness is demonstrated in two beautiful acts of God. He made us, and He redeemed us. We have been made in the image of God and bought back at a high price because God believes we are worth dying for (Hebrews 12:2). When we step onto this stone, the marvelous grace of God comes to life in a new, deeper way so that we can experience His truth.

"As for you, you were dead in your transgressions and sins, in which you used to live when you followed the ways of this world and of the ruler of the kingdom of the air, the spirit who is now at work in those who are disobedient. All of us also lived among them at one time, gratifying the cravings of our flesh and following its desires and thoughts. Like the rest, we were by nature deserving of wrath. But because of his great love for us, God, who is rich in mercy, made us alive with Christ even when we were dead in transgressions—it is by grace you have been saved. And God raised us up with Christ and seated us with him in the heavenly realms in

*Christ Jesus, in order that in the coming ages
he might show the incomparable riches of his
grace, expressed in his kindness to us in Christ
Jesus. For it is by grace you have been saved,
through faith—and this is not from yourselves,
it is the gift of God—not by works, so that no
one can boast. For we are God's handiwork,
created in Christ Jesus to do good works,
which God prepared in advance for us to do."*
Ephesians 2:1-10

Forgive me for the long Bible passage, but I think it's worth it. These truths have the transformative power to shift the course of your today, tomorrow, and forever.

DEATH (apart from God) + GRACE
(Jesus' sacrifice) = LIFE WITH CHRIST

When the pain reaches its height, when a car breaks down, when our relationships shatter, or when our physical bodies start to fail, we are faced with the sobering reminder of our inability to save ourselves. This kind of God moment allows us to accept Him and His truth. They allow us to embrace Him and trust God to work in His rightful place in our life.

Grace is one stone with two parts because at the same

time, we can be totally undeserving and completely worthy of God's love and sacrifice. When we step onto the stone of grace, our awareness of being undeserving starts to fade away. Our understanding of being worthy increases, in addition to our desire to see God be glorified. Every time I think I have used up my entire "grace allotment" from God, He showers me with more grace. Grace upon grace upon grace. This grace makes for an overwhelmingly beautiful life.

> *"The lightness of grace does not lift all*
> *the sandbags that drag the spirit down.*
> *It lightens life by removing one very*
> *dead weight in particular—*
> *the weight of anxiety about being*
> *an unacceptable person."*
> Lewis Smedes

THE NINTH STONE – HOPE

"It's going to be okay."

"When I talk to you, you always give me hope." These were the last words I ever heard from my husband. It was quite surprising, coming from the man who abandoned my daughters and me. Life's circumstances can be like a strong current that threatens to sweep us off our feet. Did you know that it only takes six inches of swiftly moving water to knock over a full-grown adult? And, if that water knocks someone down face first, they can actually drown before they have a chance to flip over.

That was me. I was beginning to be swept away by the swift moving current of bitterness, resentment, and unforgiveness in my heart. The rushing water was taking me down a dangerous and tumultuous river. In the years that passed after Steve left, those seeds of bitterness, resentment and unforgiveness began to grow and take root in my life. And if you don't learn how to process those emotions, they will eat you up.

When you hear the words "bitterness," "resentment," or "unforgiveness," who comes to mind? Whose face, or what pain, or which problem is God calling your attention to? For me, it was Steve. As I wrestled with the struggle of letting go, God gave me something to hold onto instead—hope. He did this in a very strange and beautiful way.

I heard that Steve was very sick, in the hospital, and possibly dying. God prompted me to call him, so I did. I didn't want to or feel like I had to, but I have learned that sometimes saying yes to God is the first step towards the hope we need.

Steve was in the worst place I had ever encountered him. On our phone call, he shared honestly about this low point in his life. He told me about his genuine regrets and humbly acknowledged the poor life decisions he had made.

I tried to console him. I encouraged him to reach out to the girls in a healthy way. I said, "God is giving you some extra time, so you might want to use it for good." As we continued our conversation, I spoke about God's great love for us and the salvation Jesus has purchased for us. I was amazed by the strength the Holy Spirit was giving me to stay in the moment and to point to Jesus.

There came a long pause in our conversation. I waited in silence and then heard his words in a sincere tone I had never heard before. Steve said, "When I talk to you, you always give me hope."

I clarified for him, "That's not me—that's Jesus. That's why He died on the cross—to give you hope and a future."

"But I've made some pretty dumb choices," he replied.

"We all have!" I continued, "We've all made poor choices, and that's why Jesus died for us!"

The conversation concluded shortly thereafter. I hung up the phone and a sudden rush of clear thoughts and joyful feelings overwhelmed me. For the first time, I experienced the reason why God tells us to forgive people—to release them from the grip of our hands, into God's loving arms. I experienced instantaneous liberation from my bitterness, resentment, and unforgiveness. How amazing is that? In a single phone call, those yucky feelings changed into feelings of freedom and joy!

Stepping onto the stone of hope was unlike any other stone. This stone felt like a familiar step, almost like talking with an old friend over a cup of coffee. I've always had a sense of hope in my life. I'm not entirely sure why that is—maybe it's because Jesus has always been with me. In my early years, I thought that hope was a point in time. I pictured it as some distant good in the future that beckoned me towards it. Through my life, health, and relational challenges, I slowly began to understand true hope. I learned that hope isn't a point in time, but rather a line—like a road to be walked or a journey to be explored. Now, my understanding of hope has grown even more. Hope isn't just a point, a line, or a path—it's a person. Jesus is the stone of hope. Jesus is the one who speaks to us when we are weak, doubtful, and scared. He's the one who whispers, "It's going to be okay."

"Therefore, since we have been justified through faith, we have peace with God through our Lord Jesus Christ, through whom we have gained access by faith into this grace in which we now stand. And we boast in the hope of the glory of God. Not only so, but we also glory in our sufferings, because we know that suffering produces perseverance; perseverance, character; and character, hope. And hope does not put us to shame, because God's love has been poured out into our hearts through the Holy Spirit, who has been given to us."

Romans 5:1-5

This passage can be a transfusion of hope into our souls. It encourages and reminds us that somehow, the moments, hours, and even a lifetime of suffering will eventually land on hope. And the only way suffering can find a road towards hope is if hope is a person.

If we gain something greater after suffering, we begin to see the purpose behind it. At the end of the road of suffering, if we know God deeper, see Him more clearly, and love him more dearly, then we will finally understand that our Father's plans are good. One of the frequent phrases I've adopted into my conversations and prayers is "I don't know how this is going to work, but I know God has this."

Soon after that phone call with Steve, he died. I wasn't expecting anything, but when he died, he left me the wedding ring I gave him, the Bible I gave him, and $730. These three things served as a two-fold reminder. First, of the stark finality of his death. And secondly, it was a reminder of the swift current that was carrying me along a treacherous physical and financial terrain.

Isn't it ironic that a chapter on hope would begin with a story of death? For some reason, it seems like hope and death have a bizarre connection. The concept of death, the place where some of our greatest fears about the future are found, was the proving ground for Jesus to show himself as the only legitimate and lasting source of hope—for me, for you, and for Steve.

The stone of hope is a beautiful and slippery stone. It is easy to lose our footing when the circumstances of life wash over us. Many people believe that hope is a feeling, but it's not. Hope is a person—and when we believe that, hope becomes a secure stone for us to stand on. It is on the stone of hope that we can live a great life and have beautiful, healthy relationships because we are certain that no matter what happens, "It's going to be okay."

> *"We cannot count on God to arrange what*
> *happens in our lives in ways that will make*
> *us feel good. We can, however, count on God*
> *to patiently remove all the obstacles to our*
> *enjoyment of Him. He is committed to our joy,*
> *and we can depend on Him to give us enough*
> *of a taste of that joy and enough hope that the*
> *best is still ahead to keep us going in spite of*
> *how much pain continues to plague our hearts."*
>
> Larry Crabb

THE TENTH STONE – GRATITUDE

"The desires of my heart."

*"Oh that God would give me the thing which
I long for! That before I go hence and am
no more seen, I may see a people wholly
devoted to God, crucified to the world, and
the world crucified to them. A people truly
given up to God in body, soul and substance!
How cheerfully would I then say, 'Now
lettest thou thy servant depart in peace.'"*
John Wesley

"I've got you. And through this, I'm going to show your girls who their Heavenly Father is." These tender yet powerful words that God whispered to me have been a warm blanket of security through many days of pain, tension, and strife. Desire is a tricky subject for many of us to contemplate. I figured out how to turn off the desires of my heart because few of them came into fruition. One disappointment after another chased the desires of my heart away like a scared dog with its tail between its legs. If you're anything like me, you know this struggle all too well. Have you ever shut down your desires simply because they seemed distant and impossible?

I used to read Bible verses like James 4:2, "you have not because you ask not," and sadly nod my head in agreement because I was living a "have not" kind of life. These types of verses that attempt to fan the flame of my desires would be met with a wall of reluctance. I refused to present my requests to God because I've always felt like I was the exception to verses like these. I felt like I was detached from God's possible blessings.

Through this journey of cancer and abandonment, I resisted asking for help. I just tried to work harder, figure it out on my own, and keep going. Trying to juggle teaching, music lessons, voice lessons, and church musicals as an unsupported, single mother was a fierce challenge. My girls hardly ever saw me. For some reason, I thought that at the end of all my self-sufficiency, I would get some kind of blue ribbon from God. I haven't received that blue ribbon yet, but what I have received is immeasurably more than all I could have asked for or imagined!

Even when I didn't ask for them, God poured out His blessings upon me. I really only wanted only one thing—but I received so much more. That's the kind of God our God is. When we come, He pours His presence and blessing upon us.

Without a doubt, my strongest and deepest desire has been for the life of my precious daughters. My heart's prayer has continually been, "Lord, be with my girls. Protect their hearts from the negative impact their dad's life and abandonment may have had on them. And Lord, remain close to them as I fight this cancer in my body." As I finally declared the desires of my heart, I sensed a new, fresh, and vibrant connection with God. I sensed that God and I would be working together towards these goals, spiritually fighting for the life, health, and souls of my daughters.

I love these powerful words of Scripture. These words are not theoretical—they are a practical reality. Bathing myself in God's word is one of the best decisions I've made as I've walked this difficult road. Consider His transformative words:

> *"Though you have not seen him, you*
> *love him; and even though you do not*
> *see him now, you believe in him and are*
> *filled with an inexpressible and glorious*

joy, for you are receiving the end result of
your faith, the salvation of your souls."
1 Peter 1:8-9

This passage paints an amazing portrait of a God who wants to restore us to unconditional joy and the fullness of life. On the other hand, we may have desires that run contrary to God's hopes and plans for our lives. And what kind of a Father would God be if He granted us our hearts' desires that would take us further away from Him?

As I have learned to seek Him and Him alone, God seemed to lift me up onto the stone of gratitude. He lavished blessings upon my girls and me that matched the desires of my heart.

Oh, God has blessed me in so many surprising ways! First, he has provided for our family with residuals from my days singing with Maranatha! I didn't realize that some writing and singing I did years ago could continue to be a source of support and financial blessings to my family.

Another blessing was a surprise gift from my dear friends. At a party they threw for me, my friends exclaimed, "You and your girls are going to Hawaii!!!" I was absolutely speechless. It took a while for me to get over the shock of my friends' generosity that combined to send my girls and me on a fabulous trip to Hawaii. I was blown away by this act of love and generosity from those who were closest to me.

Finally, the blessing that cemented my understanding of

God's ability to grant me the desires of my heart came when I held my first grandchild in my arms. Only a grandmother with cancer can tell you of the joy, the tears, and the gratitude that wells up in your heart when you hold a grandchild you never thought you would get to hold. God is so good! As I held and sang to this precious blessing, the words of Psalm 20:4 echoed in my head: "May he give you the desire of your heart and make all your plans succeed."

When I accepted my place as God's beloved child, it was time for a major celebration! I am so thankful for His constant and loving presence in my life. I am no longer the insecure, scared little girl who began this journey.

God picked me up and placed me on top of the stone of gratitude. On this stone, I have learned how to live differently. The blessings I received did not move me towards God. But rather, God moved me towards himself and then showered his blessings upon me by giving me the desires of my heart.

We should be astonished at
the goodness of God,
stunned that He should bother
to call us by name,
our mouths wide open at His love,
bewildered that at this very moment
we are standing on holy ground.
Brennan Manning

THE ELEVENTH STONE – PURPOSE

"God will use this."

"We resist telling a story we don't like,
and we don't like our own stories. But if
you don't like your story, then you must
not like the Author. Conversely: if you
love the Author, then you must love the
story He has written for your life."
Dan Allender

"I'm in the best place in my life, and I have cancer!" I never thought I'd say these words, much less believe them and live them out. Over the past few years, there has only been a stretch of two weeks when I wasn't doing chemotherapy, taking some new concoction, or wrestling with sickness from all the medicine. Through all of this, Jesus offered me another stone to step onto. Unlike many of the other stones, this one was not given to me to step away from something hard or challenging. Instead, it helped me step towards my purpose with God. I've always had a sense that God was using me, but it wasn't until recently that I have seen Him use all of me, and very often!

For most of my life, I misunderstood my purpose. One day I woke up and decided, "I've been thinking about my purpose all wrong." I realized with crystal clarity that my job in life is to show the people around me who our Heavenly Father really is. The more closely we listen to God and walk with Him, the more frequently God moments flow into our lives.

For some people, the thought of being close to God is terrifying. For others, including myself, God's close proximity and direction is a life-giving force that we desire more than anything else. In the Bible, King David triumphantly concluded that one day in God's presence was better than a thousand days elsewhere (Psalm 84:10).

In order to be used by God and to stand on the stone of purpose, I have learned that I need to win the "early morning battle." The early morning is what sets the course for my day. It's in the twilight of morning that I choose pity or positivity, flesh or Spirit, my work or God's work, my purpose or God's purpose. One of my favorite early morning thoughts is, "Okay

Lord, I know you are here." This phrase is my conscious choice to see and interact with the world as God intended me to. Isn't that our mission here on earth, to hallow God's name and see that his will be done (Matthew 6:9)?

Every day, every moment of our lives, we have the choice to involve ourselves in the extension of God's kingdom, or not. I was running some errands at a local Target. I overheard a heated discussion between a manager and an employee. The manager stomped off and the employee stared daggers at me as if to say, "Don't you dare come here to check out!"

I walked up anyways. The employee kept glaring at me, her eyes full of anger and hurt. It's a good thing I stepped into God's presence that morning, because otherwise I would have missed the God moment He orchestrated.

I tilted my head with a compassionate "mom look," fully equipped with the boo-boo lip. I gently asked her, "Are you okay?"

She blurted out, "No! I'm so overwhelmed!"

"I know," I responded, "Life can be really hard."

She began to soften a little. "So much is going on!" She paused. "And my hair! It's dark and curly and it used to be blonde!"

I nodded with understanding. "Is it a new style?"

She snapped back, "I'm in remission. This is the way my hair grew out after chemo."

"You're in remission! Awesome!" I replied with excitement. I paused, tugged on my wig and said, "I'm wrestling with that cancer thing, too. I can't wait till I can say, 'I'm in remission!'"

The employee closed her eyes and relaxed her body as if she were drinking in the moment. It's amazing how someone who takes a moment to connect, understand, and share empathy can move the human heart.

Then her gaze got cold and distant again. She said, "My husband said that after I get well, he's going to leave me."

Once again, I responded with empathy and compassion, "Yeah, my husband left me, too." I encouraged her, "It's going to be okay. Put your faith in God, and He will take care of you. I know what fear brings, but with Him, it'll be okay."

That same employee who had stared daggers at me five minutes earlier reached across the checkout counter and gave me a hug that seemed to last for an eternity.

To feel understood, supported, and loved is what people all around us are looking for and longing for. I told the employee I would pray for her and walked to the car with the triumphant feeling of having helped someone else find a slice of hope, joy, and peace. I love living life with God!

You can find these God moments in your own life, too. All you really need to do is to win the early morning battle. Focus your attention on God, and He'll take care of the rest.

Jesus said two amazing things about life. These two verses impart not only Jesus' purpose, but ours as well. In John 10:10, Jesus said, "I have come that they may have life, and have it to the full." Mark 10:45 says, "For even the Son of Man did not come to be served, but to serve, and to give his life as a ransom for many."

Realizing that God has a purpose not only for your life, but for every day and every hour as well, can transform a trip to Target into a divine appointment. In my clear-thinking moments, I celebrate the story God has written and is writing through my life. I often think to myself, "I'm in the best place in my life, and I have cancer!" How ironic is that??

It doesn't matter if it's blessing a waitress from Redding, encouraging a child at Stoneybrooke, or simply listening to a mom in need—I'm trying to live my life on the stone of purpose. God wants to use you today. Somehow, somewhere, He has a purpose for this day. I challenge you with a message the Holy Spirit placed deep within my soul, "God is so good. He can use this. And He will use this!"

> *"The beginning and the end of all Christian leadership is to give your life for others."*
> Henri J.M. Nouwen

The Bridge

"Oh! There you are, Jesus!"

———⟫•◦•⟪———

"Like a bridge over troubled waters..."
Paul Simon

I s it possible that our wacky experience called "life" looks better and more well-designed when we look back at it? As I mentioned earlier, God has used mental images throughout my life in very powerful ways. The picture of rushing water, stepping onto different stones, and God's provision all helped me to not only survive, but to thrive!

God blessed me with another mental image. I closed my eyes and imagined seeing Jesus face to face for the first time. I glanced back at my earthly journey, expecting to see rushing water and the individual stones which He helped me to step onto. Instead, I saw a beautiful stone bridge.

"From the end of the earth will I cry unto thee,
when my heart is overwhelmed:
lead me to the rock that is higher than I.
For thou hast been a shelter for me,
and a strong tower from the enemy."
Psalm 61:2-3

Doesn't it make sense that God's strength and refuge is more like a peaceful walk on a sturdy stone bridge, rather than trying to balance on small stones in a raging river?

One thing I do know is that the reward of following Jesus is, well, Jesus. Time will not pass the same way when we get to Heaven, but our relationship with Jesus will stay the same! The consummation of all we've hoped for and longed for will finally be realized. I'm looking forward to that day. As of right now, I am still on this side of the great divide.

> *"If I am to go on living in the body, this will mean fruitful labor for me. Yet what shall I choose? I do not know! I am torn between the two: I desire to depart and be with Christ, which is better by far; but it is more necessary for you that I remain in the body. Convinced of this, I know that I will remain, and I will continue with all of you for your progress and joy in the faith."*
> Philippians 1:22-25

Paul uses this image to reassure us that with Jesus, we have no need to fear. Romans 9:33 says, "See, I lay in Zion a stone that causes people to stumble and a rock that makes them fall, and the one who believes in him will never be put to shame." God has meaningful moments in store for us that will transform our lives and the lives of those around us. If we open our eyes, engage our hearts, and have the courage to live with God, we can live an amazing life!

You may be thinking, "God showed up for you. But how do I know that He will show up for me, too?" My response is twofold. If God showed up for me, he'll show up for anyone! And secondly, God's "showing up" has much more to do with Him than with you! It's not about what you have or haven't done. It's about Him lavishing love, forgiveness, and grace upon you. All you need to do is say "yes" to it! Receiving God and His blessings is the journey of this life. The next life is designed to create space for us to appreciate the wonder of who God is and to thank him for all the wonderful things he has done for us. I cannot wait for the day I get to see Jesus, face-to-face, and say, "Thank you!" But for now, it's just little ol' me, moving through life, *Baffled and Blessed!*

The Door

*"Death opens a door out of a little, dark
room (that's all the life we have known
before it) into a great, real place where
the true sun shines and we shall meet."*

C.S. Lewis

"Let's forget about numbers for a while. Let's just focus on the journey." These wise words from my doctor were so true. When I started my battle with cancer, my number was 1270. As the weeks passed and we explored different treatments, my mental and emotional health seemed to be tied to a cancer number.

We all do that kind of thing. We look to some measuring metric to determine if we are "okay" or not. And as my wise doctor explained, "Focusing on the numbers is the wrong approach. It's impossible to live a great life when you're constantly counting and comparing cancer numbers." That day, my doctor gave me a great gift. He gave me the freedom to focus on the right things by simply living life and remaining hopeful on my journey.

Even as I write this, I'm still hoping for a miracle. Yet,

if God chooses not to bless me in this way, I can still be thankful for the miracle of this life and promise of the next life that He's already given me. I'm still here, still hoping, still loving. He has blessed me so much!

If the trajectory of my life doesn't change, there will be an inevitable passing through the door from this realm and into the next. Of course, I'm fearful about this…mostly for my daughters. As I think about the possibility of them walking this life without me, many questions arise. "Who will share godly wisdom with them? Who will snuggle and watch movies with them? Who will they bring their tears to? How will they find their way to their loving Heavenly Father?"

As I humbly brought these questions before God, once again He reassured me of His abundant power, love, and presence. He reminded me, "I'm pretty good at loving and caring for people. I've got this covered."

Congratulations if you're still reading this section. I'm going to guess many readers stop when we begin to explore the reality of facing death. The topic of our transition from this world into the next can make cowards out of even the strongest of us. But it is in this tension that God plants His greatest messages and biggest blessings.

Some people don't think it's possible to reflect on this topic without being morbid or fearful. Yet through this process,

I have identified two essential movements in my soul: the messages I need to tell myself and the messages I want to share with my girls.

THE MESSAGES I TELL MYSELF

As I move though this adventure of life, just being becomes more and more important than doing. I can easily be overwhelmed by the thought, "What do I need to do before I go?"

When I think about who to be rather than what to do, the list simplifies itself. I move towards God's "honey do list" for me:

– Love every day.
– Always remember joy and hope.
– Capture the moments.
– Don't hold on to worries.
– Remember God's thoughts of me and for me.

This is where I spend my days. I can move more lightly, love more, be more present in relationships, and care more deeply for people than I ever have. And of course, I share tears liberally—tears of both sadness and joy. As I hold onto God's best for who He wants me to be and what he wants me to do, I can truly live the blessed life He has given me!

"If we kept in mind that we will soon inevitably die, our lives would be completely different. If a person knows that he will die in a half hour, he certainly will not bother doing trivial, stupid, or, especially, bad things during this half hour. Perhaps you have half a century before you die—what makes this any different from a half hour?"
Leo Tolstoy

THE MESSAGES I WANT TO PASS ON TO MY GIRLS

When I close my eyes and think about the messages I want to be sealed in the hearts and minds of my sweet daughters, I want them to hear and remember this:

"I love you! I am so proud of you! You're going to be okay! I can't wait to see you again! God is powerful and will continue to meet your needs and give you so much more!"

These words come with a mix of tears, deep emotion, and lots of exclamation points! All of this is because I am passionate about my girls. I am utterly convinced that they are in the hands of a good and loving God, and that He who began this journey in and with them will be faithful to see it through to the end (Philippians 1:6).

> *"There are only two lasting bequests*
> *we can hope to give our children.*
> *One of these is roots, the other, wings."*
> Johann Wolfgang von Goethe

I have been so inspired by Paul's bold and courageous words:

> *When the perishable has been*
> *clothed with the imperishable,*
> *and the mortal with immortality,*
> *then the saying that is written will come true:*
> *"Death has been swallowed up in victory."*
> I Corinthians 15:54

Death doesn't have the final word—God does. Passing from this existence to the next is something that God has been leading people through for thousands of years. It's a door. It's a beautiful door that leads to a realm of relational experience and fulfillment that surpasses our imagination. Consider these words from a renowned evangelist as he spoke on the topic of his passing:

"Someday you will read in the papers that D. L. Moody, of East Northfield, is dead. Don't you believe a word of it! At that moment I shall be more alive than I am now. I shall have gone up higher, that is all; out of this old clay tenement into a house that is immortal—a body that death cannot touch; that sin cannot taint; a body fashioned like unto His glorious body."
D. L. Moody

D. L. Moody knew. I know. I hope that you will also know and experience that God has it all under control. The best is yet to come!

"Jesus didn't come to explain away or remove our suffering, He came to fill it with His presence."
Paul Claudel

Editor's Note

Debbie Owens walked through the door on September 25, 2018. She wasn't able to see the final copy of this book that she poured herself into. But she knew that God gave her a life and a story–both of which needed to be shared with those who are willing to hear. And right now, she's enjoying the presence of her Heavenly Father, probably singing and certainly smiling.

About Sophia

Sophia Morris was born and raised in Southern California. She has been blessed with many opportunities to learn from wonderful people like Debbie Owens. Sophia attended Stoneybrooke Christian School. Through music classes, chapels, and musical performances at Stoneybrooke, God used Debbie Owens to inspire, encourage, and leave God's imprint on a young Sophia. After Stoneybrooke, Sophia attended Santa Margarita Catholic High School where she was given the opportunity to be challenged and to grow in both academics and athletics. Sophia is currently a student at Biola University, where she is studying psychology and running track. Following Debbie Owens' example, she loves to encourage and inspire others as she seeks to glorify God in everything.

Sophia can also be found at http://www.inspirebysophia.com.

.